American CULTURE & CONFLICT

Living Through The Revolutionary War

Clara MacCarald

Rourke
Educational Media
rourkeeducationalmedia.com

Before Reading:

Building Academic Vocabulary and Background Knowledge

Before reading a book, it is important to tap into what your child or students already know about the topic. This will help them develop their vocabulary, increase their reading comprehension, and make connections across the curriculum.

1. Look at the cover of the book. What will this book be about?
2. What do you already know about the topic?
3. Let's study the Table of Contents. What will you learn about in the book's chapters?
4. What would you like to learn about this topic? Do you think you might learn about it from this book? Why or why not?
5. Use a reading journal to write about your knowledge of this topic. Record what you already know about the topic and what you hope to learn about the topic.
6. Read the book.
7. In your reading journal, record what you learned about the topic and your response to the book.
8. After reading the book complete the activities below.

Content Area Vocabulary

Read the list. What do these words mean?

artisans

boycott

committees

enlist

enslaved

intolerable

loyalists

militias

patriots

repeal

After Reading:

Comprehension and Extension Activity

After reading the book, work on the following questions with your child or students in order to check their level of reading comprehension and content mastery.

1. In what ways did ordinary colonists protest the British before the war started? (Summarize)
2. How did people know which side their neighbors were on? (Infer)
3. How did committees look for people who supported Britain before the war? (Asking Questions)
4. What are some ways your life is different from a person living during the Revolutionary War? (Text to Self Connection)
5. Why did the Sons of Liberty destroy tea during the Boston Tea Party? (Asking Questions)

Extension Activity

Research a colonist who lived during the Revolutionary War. Was the person a patriot or a loyalist? Why? Pretend to write a diary entry for the colonist talking about how the war affected their life.

Table of Contents

Key Events

February 10, 1763:	The Treaty of Paris of 1763 ends the Seven Years' War
October 7, 1763:	King George III issues the Proclamation of 1763, limiting settlement on American Indian land
March 22, 1765:	The British Parliament passes the Stamp Act to raise money from the colonies
March 18, 1766:	Parliament repeals the Stamp Act
March 5, 1770:	British soldiers fire on an angry crowd and kill five colonists, an event called the Boston Massacre
December 16, 1773:	At the Boston Tea Party, colonists dump tea into Boston Harbor to protest the tea tax
September 5, 1774:	The First Continental Congress begins meeting
April 19, 1775:	British soldiers and American militiamen clash at the Battles of Lexington and Concord, beginning the Revolutionary War
November 7, 1775:	Lord Dunmore's Proclamation offers freedom to enslaved people leaving patriot slaveholders to fight for the British
July 4, 1776:	Congress adopts the Declaration of Independence
February 6, 1778:	France enters the war by signing a treaty with the United States
October 19, 1781:	British forces surrender at Yorktown, Virginia, ending most of the fighting
September 3, 1783:	America and Britain sign the Treaty of Paris of 1783 to end the Revolutionary War
September 17, 1789:	Delegates sign the U.S. Constitution

CHAPTER ONE

British Colonies

Some settlers disregarded the Proclamation Line and continued to clash with American Indians in the lands won by Britain in the Seven Years' War.

When Britain won the Seven Years' War in 1763, people living in the 13 colonies saw themselves as British. As the events of the American Revolution unfolded, the colonists would become Americans.

The Treaty of Paris in 1763 gave French and Spanish land in North America to Britain. Colonists wanted to settle this land, or buy it to sell for profit. But conflict with American Indians persuaded King George III of England to make the Proclamation of 1763, which banned settlers from moving west of the Appalachian Mountains.

George Washington not only bought and sold land, he sometimes worked as a surveyor. He determined the boundaries for his own or other people's properties.

LAND FOR PROFIT

George Washington (1732-1799) had a direct interest in the Proclamation Line. He and other colonists who fought in the Seven Years' War were promised land behind the line. Although Washington owned farms, he made lots of money buying and selling land, starting with 1,459 acres (590 hectares) in Virginia.

Colonists hated the new law. Land was important because many colonists were farmers. Others were merchants or **artisans**. Businesses struggled after the war. They had few customers. Colonists had very little British money, but Parliament made colonial paper money illegal.

Even though colonists were struggling, Parliament passed laws to tax the colonies to help pay for their protection. One, the Stamp Act of 1765, required buying a stamp on all printed material. Most colonists would be affected. For example, anyone who wanted a newspaper, a legal paper, or playing cards would have to pay the tax.

The Stamp Act required anything printed in the colonies to be printed on paper with an official stamp such as this one.

NEWS SPREADS THROUGH THE COLONIES

Colonists didn't have the Internet, but they did have printing presses. These presses printed weekly newspapers and pamphlets. Newspapers helped colonists keep up with events. Pamphlets, which consisted of folded paper, told people what to think about those events. Hundreds of pamphlets argued about the rights of the colonists.

In colonial taverns and homes, people discussed the stamp taxes. Colonists voted for their own assemblies, but they didn't vote for representatives to Parliament. Many colonists thought Parliament had no right to tax them.

In most places, only white male property owners who were 21 or older could vote. Sometimes the vote was only given to followers of certain religions.

Nine of the colonial assemblies sent delegates to the Stamp Act Congress, which declared that there should be no taxation without representation.

COLONIAL ELECTIONS

Colonial governments had three parts: a governor, a council, and an assembly. While the British appointed the governor and council members, the colonists themselves voted for members of the assembly. The assemblies began to claim only they had the right to tax the colonists.

Governors such as William Shirley (1694-1771), appointed to lead Massachusetts, answered to the king.

As anger grew, colonists began a **boycott** of British trade. People formed groups to oppose the taxes and took to the streets to protest. Anger united colonists who normally wouldn't work together. The colonists forced Parliament to **repeal** the unpopular Stamp Act, but Parliament still believed they had the right to control the colonies.

After Parliament repealed the Stamp Act, they passed the Declaratory Act. This act said Parliament had the right to make laws regarding the colonies.

British officials asked for military help collecting taxes in Boston. In 1770, the soldiers fired on an angry mob, killing five colonists. Colonists called it the Boston Massacre.

A DEMAND FOR FREEDOM

Enslaved colonists were even more hungry for freedom than free colonists. In 1766, a crowd of enslaved people marched in Charleston, South Carolina, calling for liberty. Free colonists were terrified, even though they had recently celebrated the very same thing. Throughout the Revolution, slaveholders feared their enslaved people would stage an uprising.

CHAPTER TWO

Dawn of the Revolution

In 1773, a protest by a Sons of Liberty group against the Tea Act became the Boston Tea Party. Parliament passed laws to punish Massachusetts, which the colonists called the **Intolerable** Acts. The laws closed the Boston harbor and ended local elections in Massachusetts, replacing local rule with a royal governor.

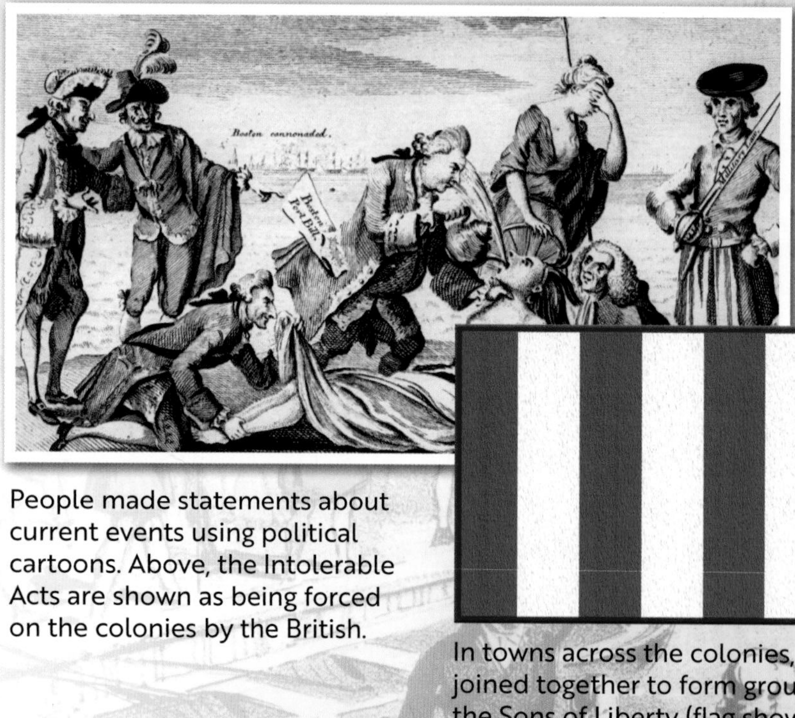

People made statements about current events using political cartoons. Above, the Intolerable Acts are shown as being forced on the colonies by the British.

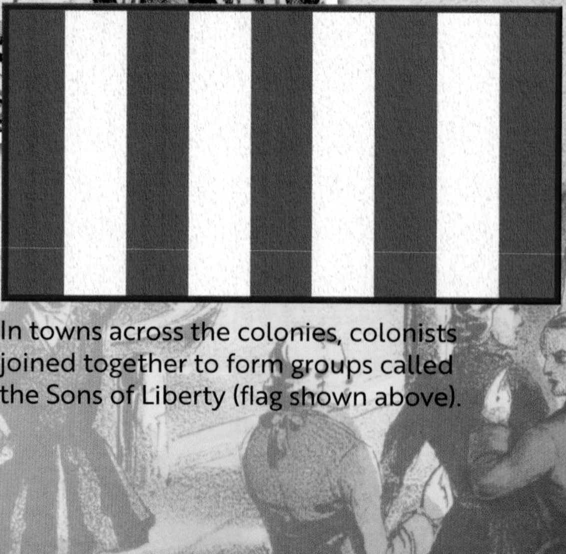

In towns across the colonies, colonists joined together to form groups called the Sons of Liberty (flag shown above).

COLONIAL TEA

American colonists spent a lot of money on the tea trade. Women would host friends to tea and show off their fancy tea-making tools. To protest the Tea Act, people publicly destroyed their own tea. The Sons of Liberty led other tea parties, not just the famous Boston Tea Party.

People throughout the 13 colonies felt under attack. All summer, colonists flocked to meetings with their neighbors. At these meetings, people chose representatives to attend larger conventions. From each colony, conventions sent delegates to the First Continental Congress. The colonies were acting united.

Georgia was the only colony of the 13 not to send delegates to the First Continental Congress. They were in the middle of a conflict with American Indians.

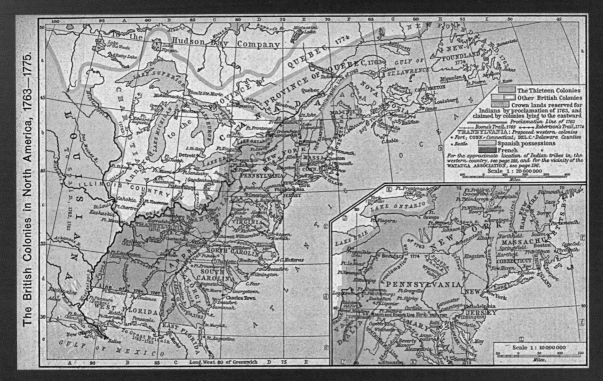

The Quebec Act added land west of the 13 colonies (left of the pink and green areas on the map) to the colony of Quebec. This territory was desired by other colonists.

THE QUEBEC ACT

Not all of the Intolerable Acts punished Massachusetts. The Quebec Act reshaped Canada. Britain gained Canada from France after the Seven Years' War. Many colonists were French. The act allowed them to keep French law and religion while adding land west of the Appalachian Mountains to Canada.

The British hoped to gain support from the colonists in Quebec with the Quebec Act.

Congress declared another boycott. Colonists began creating **committees** to oversee the boycott in their local area. Committee members included workers, artisans, and small farmers as well as rich men. Ordinary people took control of their own communities.

The colonies had very little manufacturing ability. But natural resources such as wood were more plentiful than in England.

Men use traditional colonial woodworking methods.

A man reenacts colonial woodworking methods. Goods made by the colonists tended to be made and used locally rather than traded with distant towns.

The committees began to change colonial life. To lessen the need for British goods, they encouraged people to manufacture goods at home. They promoted simple living to avoid waste. By spying on their neighbors, committee members searched for people who supported the British.

THE REVOLUTION WILL NOT HAVE DANCING

The committees thought a simple life contained more virtue and less waste. They wanted colonists to dress and act more simply. Many communities banned gambling, playing cards, horseracing, and dancing. Taverns and individuals were warned not to hold balls or otherwise allow public dancing.

Men reenact a Revolutionary War battle. Since the beginning of settlement, able-bodied white men were often expected to help defend the colonies along with soldiers.

As the committees took power, the colonial governments supported by Britain lost power. Local **militias** started answering only to the committees. The colonists realized they might need to defend themselves. Committees and militias began to gather weapons around the colonies.

Colonists took pride in wearing fabrics made at home.

BUSY BEES

Colonists in the cities were used to buying things they needed, not making them. With the boycott, that changed. It became fashionable to learn to spin wool into yarn, for example. Spinning bees gave women a chance to publicly support the resistance. Women competed over who could spin the most.

No one knows which side fired the first shot at the Battle of Lexington.

On April 19, 1775, the British attempted to seize a store of military weapons in Concord, Massachusetts, and instead clashed with a colonial militia. When word of the battle spread, colonists in other colonies wanted to help Massachusetts. The Battles of Lexington and Concord became the first battles of the American Revolution.

CHAPTER THREE

Divided Loyalties

Congress took charge of the fighting, creating the Continental Army. On July 4, 1776, Congress declared independence from Britain. To pay for the war, Congress issued Continental currency. Colonists could again use local money, although the value of that money would go down over time.

Young, single men without property could hope to gain money or land by joining the Continental Army.

The new commander in chief, Washington, hoped to turn his Continental Army into a force as orderly and well-trained as his British foes.

From 1775 to 1779, Congress issued over 200 million dollars in Continental currency.

NOT WORTH A CONTINENTAL

Continental currency celebrated the Revolution, showing soldiers or eagles rather than the British king. Unfortunately, people need to trust paper money for it to have worth. Congress was broke. To make matters worse, British forces spread fake money. As the years went on, Congress had to admit Continentals were worthless.

Each colony began to create a state government based on the idea of rule by the people, for the people—although this mostly meant white men with property. People traveled from the countryside to the towns for election days.

Election days were often treated like festivals with food, drink, and parades.

In Windsor, Vermont, on July 8, 1777, delegates declared Vermont's independence from New York by signing a new state constitution.

CONSTITUTIONAL FREEDOM

When Vermont adopted its state constitution in 1777, it became the first state to ban slavery, although only of adults. In 1780, the Massachusetts constitution declared that all men were born free. Three years later, a court ruled that the state had therefore banned slavery.

Vermont State Archives

Like other state constitutions, the Vermont Constitution specified the structure of the state's government.

The state constitutions tended to limit the power of the state governments. Seven specifically included a bill of rights for their citizens.

Neighbors gathered, socializing and conducting business. They voted for delegates to the state conventions, which wrote the state constitutions. Voters approved the finished constitutions and elected government officials.

THE FIRST CONTINENTAL CONGRESS · 1774

~OUR GOVERNMENT~
CONCEIVED IN FREEDOM
AND PURCHASED WITH BLOOD
CAN BE PRESERVED ONLY BY CONSTANT VIGILANCE
WILLIAM JENNINGS BRYAN 1908

Patriots felt determined and hopeful even though the Continental Army suffered several defeats. The British also captured important cities such as New York, New York, and Philadelphia, Pennsylvania.

WAR OF WORDS

Newspapers could also take sides. Sometimes the printers had to flee the fighting, or were shut down by the opposite side. New papers popped up, or old ones went back into production when or where it was safe to do so.

America was forging a new path, but not everyone agreed with the new direction. **Patriots** supported independence from the homeland. About two out of five colonists may have been patriots. **Loyalists** supported England. A fifth of colonists may have been loyalists. The rest of the colonists did not want to take sides. They just wanted to stay home and run their businesses or farms without being bothered.

Some patriots tarred and feathered loyalists or British officials to shame them.

Both Americans and the British forced people to swear loyalty oaths. In areas controlled by the patriots, they took property from loyalists, sometimes selling it to raise money for the Revolution. Loyalists were banned from holding public office and sometimes chased out of their homes by the patriots.

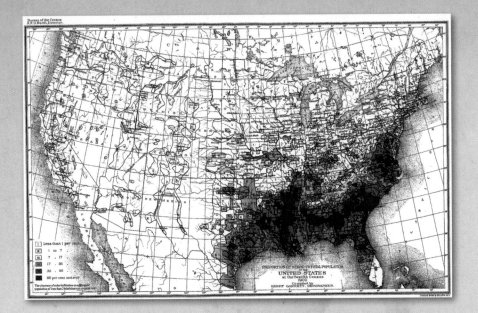

Many loyalists fled to the cities held by British soldiers. More than 20,000 loyalist men took up arms to fight against the patriots. Some African Americans were patriots, while thousands of enslaved people tried to gain freedom by running away and fighting in the British army.

Surrounded by a patriot mob, loyalists would have little choice but to sign a loyalty oath to the Americans.

DUNMORE'S PROCLAMATION

After fleeing Virginia, Royal Governor John Murray, also known as the Fourth Earl of Dunmore (1730-1809), made a proclamation. Any enslaved person in Virginia held by patriots who left their master to fight for the British would be freed. Soon, hundreds of African Americans began signing up. The proclamation angered many slaveholders.

CHAPTER FOUR

A Land at War

Armies ranged across the colonies. More than 200,000 men fought at different times in the Continental Army. With many husbands leaving home to **enlist**, some wives took on more responsibility. They learned to run farms and businesses while continuing to take care of their family's home life. Patriot men who stayed home often belonged to local militias.

Militias supported the Continental Army, although Washington and others did not always trust their courage.

THE MILITIA

More than 145,000 patriots served as part of a militia during the war. At home, sometimes a militia kept order in the community. When a militia was called up to fight, they might leave for a few months at a time. The training and experience of militiamen varied greatly.

The conflict destroyed houses, farms, and businesses. The poor conditions found in many army camps encouraged diseases, which soldiers then spread to the rest of the population. Even far from the official armies, groups of patriots and loyalists attacked each other.

Soldiers had more than bullets to worry about. Food and clothing were often in short supply and of poor quality.

reenactors

The British saw patriots as traitors. They kept prisoners of war in terrible conditions.

Colonists could make money by supplying the British or American armies, but often soldiers took what they needed without paying. Many women and children who lost their homes to war followed the American army. They made a living by washing and cooking for soldiers.

Some women fought in Revolutionary battles, but many more worked behind the scenes. They provided services and took care of wounded soldiers.

BATTLING A SMALL BUT DEADLY POX

The smallpox virus killed hundreds of thousands of people during the Revolution. To gain immunity, people would put material containing the virus into a cut. Often they'd get a mild case of the disease. Those who survived were safe from smallpox.

INDIAN ATTACK ON THE VILLAGE OF SAINT LOUIS 1780

American Indian groups fought in battles alongside patriots or loyalists as well as attacking on their own. Some American Indians joined a specific militia or an army.

Patriots feared more than just the British and loyalists. Slaveholders feared that their enslaved people would revolt against them. Near the frontier, colonists feared attacks from American Indians. Some tribes, such as the Oneidas, fought for the patriots. Others, such as the Shawnees, supported the British because they knew that the colonists wanted to settle on their land.

To bring trade goods to the patriots, ships had to avoid the Royal Navy and British-held ports.

Many goods, from soap to clothing, became scarce as the war disrupted trade. The country had few roads or bridges. The British controlled many American ports, making trade between patriots and other countries difficult.

Benjamin Franklin
1706 - 1790

AN AMERICAN OVERSEAS

Benjamin Franklin spent much of the war in France, starting at age 70. He purposefully dressed in simple clothes. Franklin charmed French society with his appearance and his intelligence. He persuaded them to not only ally with the Americans, but also to lend America a large amount of money.

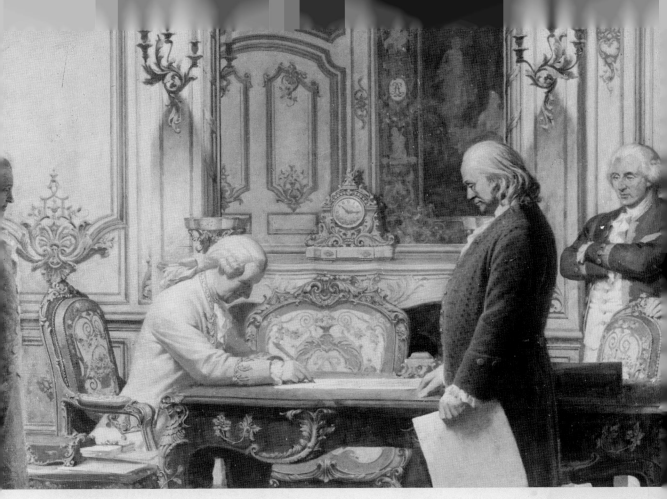

France and Spain still resented having lost the Seven Years' War to Britain.

In 1778, France signed two treaties of formal support with America. One promised French and Spanish help in the war. The other created a trade relationship. More trade goods began to arrive, although many supplies from France ended up with the army.

CHAPTER FIVE

A Revolutionary Peace

The British army surrendered to American forces at Yorktown, Virginia, on October 19, 1781. Most fighting ended. America and Britain finally signed the Treaty of Paris in 1783, ending the Revolutionary War. Soldiers from the Continental Army headed home to rebuild their lives.

The 1783 Treaty of Paris carved up North America among the United States, Britain, and Spain, ignoring American Indian land rights.

In states such as Massachusetts, some taxes went to support churches.

RELIGIONS IN THE STATES

Americans followed many different religions. Christians might be Protestants, Catholics, or something else. Some colonists were Jewish. Enslaved people might be Muslim or follow an African religion. Some states protected religious freedom, but in some places people who practiced some religions couldn't vote or hold office.

Many ministers took sides and aided the war effort. The Reverend James Caldwell (1734-1781) (above) carried out religious and worldly duties for the patriots' army.

Both the British and the Americans agreed to repay property or money owed to people belonging to the other side. But both sides found it difficult to keep this promise. The patriots had used a lot of loyalist property to help pay for the war. No one wanted to give it back to people they saw as enemies.

Mary Brant (1736-1796) of the Mohawks helped convince many fellow Haudenosaunee to support the British. Her brother Joseph (1743-1807) (above) was a Mohawk leader. Both siblings settled in Ontario after the war.

Some loyalists took their cases to court, trying to recover their property.

The British had hoped to harm the colonists by offering their enslaved people freedom. Tens of thousands of African Americans joined the British, while about 5,000 fought on the partriot side.

NEW HOMES

Not all enslaved people who fought for the British found freedom, but thousands made it out of America after the war. Many white loyalists created new homes in Canada, but African Americans were treated poorly. Many left and settled in the West African nation of Sierra Leone.

Settlers found hard work as well as disease and other dangers at Sierra Leone.

Several of America's Founding Fathers were slaveholders, including Washington and Thomas Jefferson (1743-1826).

Meanwhile, the Americans wanted enslaved people who had escaped to the British side to be returned to slaveholders, because they considered enslaved people to be property. British officials managed to transport thousands of African-American loyalists out of America. Thousands more never escaped slavery, ending up enslaved either in America or in other British colonies.

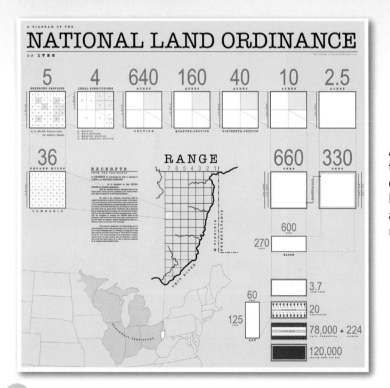

After the war, Congress ordered the Northwest Territories to be divided into six-mile-wide (9.66 kilometer) squares. Congress also set up a system for creating new states.

1768 Boundary Line Treaty Map

American Indian Lands

Fort Stanwix
Boundary Line

Colonial Lands

Treaty of Hard Labor

1763 King's
Proclamation

Settlers began moving west of the Appalachians during the war. With the treaty, Britain gave up its claim to this land to the Americans. The movement of settlers would quickly grow, with thousands of people pouring onto American Indian lands.

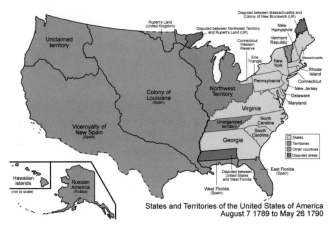

In 1790, much of the land which would become the modern United States was still controlled by other nations and groups.

CLAIMING NEW LAND

The United States signed several treaties with American Indian groups after the war. At Fort Stanwix in 1784, the Haudenosaunee Confederacy gave up land west of the Ohio River. But tribes such as the Delaware and the Shawnee thought they owned this land, not the Haudenosaunee.

CHAPTER SIX

Echoes of Revolution

Despite the challenges faced by the new nation, the patriots celebrated. They had defeated the mightiest army and navy in the world. Everywhere in America, people discussed what freedom meant, how to be virtuous, and how to create a new, democratic society.

In 1861, Henry Wadsworth Longfellow (1807-1882) published the poem "Paul Revere's Ride" about a Revolutionary War hero. Though stirring, it didn't stick to the facts.

The Americans won famous victories at Trenton, New Jersey, and Saratoga, New York. They forced the British to recognize their independence.

The heroes and events of the Revolution became legends. People celebrated the values of their new nation in magazines, books, and plays.

Weems's stories became American fables.

Mason L. Weems
1759 – 1825

TELLING STORIES

Parson Mason Locke Weems wrote about many famous Americans. A year after Washington died, Weems wrote a biography about him. Weems was known to write tall tales. Stories like Washington chopping down his father's cherry tree probably weren't true, but Americans loved them.

Some people asked why they didn't have a place in the government. After women's experiences during the Revolution, they continued to take part in public life. Still, almost all states denied women the vote.

The first New Jersey constitution allowed both women and African Americans to vote if they were free and had enough money. Married women still couldn't vote, because legally their husband owned everything in the family. Both groups lost the right to vote in New Jersey in 1807.

After decades of work, American women finally gained the right to vote in 1920 with the passing of the Nineteenth Amendment.

Abigail Adams (1744-1818) wrote a famous letter to her husband John telling him to "remember the ladies" as he helped create the new government.

In 1793, Congress passed a Fugitive
Slave Act. It required the authorities
to return runaways to slavery.

Many enslaved people freed
themselves during the war, either
by escaping or by fighting in either
army. Northern states began to
slowly ban slavery. But other states,
especially those whose plantations
relied on slave labor, ignored the
demands by enslaved people for
liberty. In most states, laws limited
the rights of free African Americans.
Freedom wasn't equality.

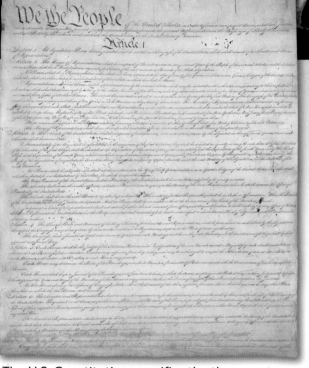

The U.S. Constitution was signed on September 17, 1787.

The U.S. Constitution specifies the three parts of the U.S. government and the powers held by each.

After fighting the British government, many Americans wanted their new governments to be weak. Eventually, though, the challenges America faced after the war would lead to granting the federal government more power through the U.S. Constitution, which still governs the United States.

FOURTH OF JULY

The first celebration of the Declaration of Independence was in Philadelphia, Pennsylvania, on July 8, 1776, four days after it was approved by Congress. In 1777, Philadelphia marked July 4 with bells, bonfires, and fireworks. The tradition spread across the country. In 1870, Congress made Independence Day a holiday.

The victory of the Continental Army against its larger foe also inspired struggles for freedom in other countries. The first shot fired at the Battles of Lexington and Concord became known as "the shot heard round the world." The Revolution also inspired Americans over the years to protest their own government to protect their own rights. Without the Revolution, there would be no America as it exists today.

Battle of Lexington.

Bureau, Engraving & Printing.

There's no proof that Betsy Ross (1752-1836) sewed the first U.S. flag. Beginning with 13 stars and 13 stripes, the number of stars would change to match the number of states.

The phrase "shot heard round the world" came from a poem written by Ralph Waldo Emerson (1803-1882).

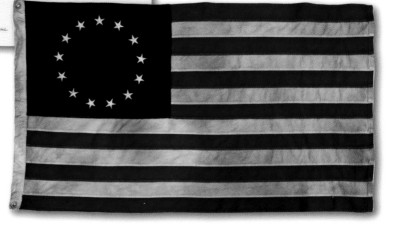

Glossary

artisans (AHR-ti-zuhns): people who craft things by hand

boycott (BOI-kaht): refusing to do business with someone or to buy something as a protest

committees (kuh-MIT-tees): groups of people chosen to take charge of something

enlist (en-LIST): to join the military

enslaved (en-SLAVED): held in a condition of slavery

intolerable (in-TAH-lur-uh-buhl): too much to endure

loyalists (LOI-uhl-ists): colonists who stayed loyal to Britain

militias (muh-LISH-uhs): groups of citizens who are ready and able to fight but who are not in the regular military

patriots (PAY-tree-uhts): colonists who supported American independence

repeal (ri-PEEL): to get rid of a law

Index

Show What You Know

1. Why was the Proclamation Line of 1763 important to the colonists?

2. How did the colonists start taking control of their own communities after the Intolerable Acts?

3. What were some of the reasons people supported the British?

4. What were some ways the fighting of the Revolution affected people who stayed home?

5. How did the end of the Revolutionary War affect Americans?

Further Reading

Howell, Sara, *What Caused the American Revolution?*,
   Gareth Stevens, 2017.

Murray, Stuart, *American Revolution (DK Eyewitness Books)*,
   DK Children, 2015.

Thompson, Ben, *Guts & Glory: The American Revolution*,
   Little Brown Books for Young Readers, 2017.

About the Author

Clara MacCarald is a children's book author with a master's degree in biology. She lives with her family in an off-grid house nestled in the forests of central New York. When not parenting her daughter, she spends her time writing nonfiction books for kids.

www.rourkeeducationalmedia.com

Photo Credits: Cover: courtesy of the National Guard; PG4-5; The National Archives-Public Domain, Courtesy Library of Congress-Public Domain. PG6-7; vgoodrich-shutterstock.com, fotomixer, The US National Archives. PG8-9; John Trumbull-Public Domain, slavazyryanov, Thomas Hudson. PG10-11; us.mil, Courtesy Library of Congress-Pub. Domain. PG12-13; Courtesy Library of Congress-Pub. Domain, PG14-15; T.H. Matheson, The US National Archives, Pbjamesphoto. PG16-17; Ritu Manoj Jethani, Travel Bug-shutterstock.com. PG18-19; n4 PhotoVideo-shutterstock.com, alexey anashkin, 1903 by John H. Daniels & Son, Boston. PG20-21; Engraving by H.W. after Howard Pyle, 1881-82, Courtesy Library of Congress-Pub Domain. PG22-23; Rui Serra Maia, Adair Mulligan, Vermont Historical Society. PG24-25; Archibald MacNeal Willard, The US National Archives. PG26-27; The US National Archives-Pub Domain. PG28-29; sphraner, F.C. Yohn. PG30-31; cabania, Courtesy Library of Congress-Pub Domain PG32-33; Everett Historical. PG34-35: National Archives. PG36-37; The US National Archives. PG38-39; Everett Historical, Golbez (Multi-license with GFDL and Creative Commons CC-BY 2.5). PG40-41; H.W. Longfellow (1868), John Trumbull, Grant Wood. PG42-43; Eastman Johnson, The US National Archives. PG44-45; Howard Chandler Christy, Courtesy Library of Congress-Pub Domain. Stock.com, shutterstock.com. Wikipedia.com CCA-Share Alike 2.0, 3.0, International.

Edited by: Keli Sipperley

Produced by Blue Door Education for Rourke Educational Media. Cover and Interior design by: Jennifer Dydyk

Living Through the Revolutionary War / Clara MacCarald
(American Culture and Conflict)
  ISBN 978-1-64156-414-4 (hard cover)
  ISBN 978-1-64156-540-0 (soft cover)
  ISBN 978-1-64156-663-6 (e-Book)
Library of Congress Control Number: 2018930434

Rourke Educational Media

Printed in the United States of America, North Mankato, Minnesota